Connections!

MONEY

CAROLINE GRIMSHAW

TEXT EDITOR
IQBAL HUSSAIN

CONSULTANT
DR JANE COLLIER

JUDGE INSTITUTE OF MANAGEMENT STUDIES, UNIVERSITY OF CAMBRIDGE

ILLUSTRATIONS
NICK DUFFY ☆ SPIKE GERRELL ☆ JO MOORE

TWOCAN

in association with
FRANKLIN WATTS

Connections!

MONEY

CREATIVE AND EDITORIAL DIRECTOR
CONCEPT/FORMAT/DESIGN/TEXT
CAROLINE GRIMSHAW

TEXT EDITOR
IQBAL HUSSAIN

CONSULTANT
DR JANE COLLIER
JUDGE INSTITUTE OF MANAGEMENT STUDIES, UNIVERSITY OF CAMBRIDGE

ILLUSTRATIONS
NICK DUFFY ☆ **SPIKE GERRELL**
JO MOORE

THANKS TO
LAURA CARTWRIGHT PICTURE RESEARCH
BRONWEN LEWIS EDITORIAL SUPPORT
AND **ANDREW JARVIS** ☆ **TIM SANPHER**
CHARLES SHAAR MURRAY

TITLES IN THIS SERIES →
☆ PEOPLE
☆ BUILDINGS
☆ EARTH
☆ ART
☆ MUSIC
☆ MACHINES
☆ MONEY

CONCEIVED AND DESIGNED BY CAROLINE GRIMSHAW FOR
TWO-CAN PUBLISHING LTD
346 OLD STREET
LONDON EC1V 9NQ

THIS EDITION PUBLISHED BY TWO-CAN PUBLISHING LTD IN 1997
IN ASSOCIATION WITH
FRANKLIN WATTS
96 LEONARD STREET
LONDON EC2A 4RH

HARDBACK ISBN 1-85434-433-1 PAPERBACK ISBN 1-85434-434-X
DEWEY DECIMAL CLASSIFICATION 332.4

HARDBACK 2 4 6 8 10 9 7 5 3 1
A CATALOGUE RECORD FOR THIS BOOK IS AVAILABLE
FROM THE BRITISH LIBRARY.

PRINTED IN HONG KONG.

Contents

DISCOVER THE CONNECTIONS THROUGH QUESTIONS AND ANSWERS...
YOU CAN READ THIS BOOK FROM START TO FINISH OR
LEAP-FROG THROUGH THE SECTIONS
FOLLOWING THE PATHS SUGGESTED
IN THESE SPECIAL 'CONNECT!' BOXES.

Connect!

*ENJOY YOUR JOURNEY OF
DISCOVERY AND UNDERSTANDING*

Metal, paper, plastic – what is

money

and why do we have it?

What are some of the strangest forms of money?

Who invented paper money?

Why do coins have pictures on them?

You'll find all these questions (and more!)
answered in PART ONE of your journey of discovery
and understanding. Turn the page! ---->

1 Metal, paper, plastic – what is money?

Money can be anything at all, as long as it is accepted as a form of payment. It can then be exchanged for goods or services.

Connect!

DOES EVERYONE USE SOME KIND OF MONEY? SEE Q3.

1 MONEY CAN BE EXCHANGED FOR SOMETHING YOU WANT

☆ I WANT A CLEAN CAR.

☆ I WANT A NEW BOOK.

● The man exchanges money for a 'service' – a task that someone carries out for him.

● The boy performs the service and exchanges some of what he earns for 'goods', in this case a book.

2 MONEY HELPS US TO WORK OUT WHAT SOMETHING IS WORTH

Just as we use hours to measure time and kilometres to measure distance, so we use money to measure value.

☆ THIS DIAMOND RING IS WORTH £1,000.

☆ THIS PLASTIC RING IS WORTH £1.

3 MONEY CAN BE SAVED AND USED TO BUY SOMETHING IN THE FUTURE

People use money to store their wealth. They may save it in a bank, or use it to invest in gold, jewellery, paintings, property and even businesses.

Prove It!

Make a list of all the things that you buy with your pocket money. How many are goods and how many are services?

Connect!

CAN MONEY BECOME WORTHLESS? SEE Q38.

2 Has there always been money?

Thousands of years ago, people realised that some items, such as animal skins and things made of gold and silver, could be exchanged for something that they needed or wanted. This exchange gradually led to the development of the money we use today.

☆ USING PRECIOUS METALS

About 4,500 years ago, in ancient Mesopotamia (now a region in Iraq), people paid for what they wanted using pieces of precious metals, such as gold and silver.

⬆ This stone tablet was made in Mesopotamia between 1865 BC and 1804 BC. It is one of the earliest written records of money being used.

The ancient Egyptians also made payments with gold, silver and copper. The metal was cut into bars, rings or strips. The actual shape was unimportant – it was the weight that mattered.

Can people survive without money?

Today, most societies use money to buy things. But a few still use an early form of trade known as barter. No money changes hands – instead, goods or services are swapped for other goods or services.

☆ HOW BARTER WORKS

In countries such as Africa, Asia and South America, families may produce enough food to support themselves. To obtain any food or goods they cannot grow or make, they must swap, or barter, what they have for what they want. A successful barter takes place when the supply of goods meets the demand.

☆ THE PROBLEMS WITH BARTER

● Bartering can only take place when the person who wants to swap, say, a cow for some corn, finds a farmer with corn who needs a cow. Finding the right person may be time-consuming.

● Both parties need to agree on how much each good or service is worth. But how many pails of corn are equal to one cow? Haggling can take time and may even result in the exchange being cancelled.

In the late 19th century, a French singer called Mademoiselle Zelie performed on an island in the Pacific Ocean, where they still used barter. She was paid with pigs, poultry and fruit. This payment could not very easily be swapped for anything that the singer wanted!

Connect!

WHY DO CHINESE PEOPLE SOMETIMES BURN MONEY? FIND OUT IN Q15.

Connect!

WHAT OTHER STRANGE FORMS OF MONEY HAVE THERE BEEN? CHECK OUT Q5.

Chinese traders weighed out gold and silver ingots using hand balances. The Chinese people used ingots as a form of money up until the 1930s. The ingot pictured right weighs one liang (ounce). The heaviest Chinese ingots weighed up to 50 liangs each.

Prove It!

You can weigh out any quantity from 1 to 127 using just seven weights - 1, 2, 4, 8, 16, 32 and 64. For example, 7=1+2+4. Which combinations of weights do you need to measure 26, 75 and 118?
THE ANSWERS ARE HIDDEN ON THIS PAGE.

Does the world need money?

The world needs something that most people recognise as valuable and agree to accept in return for goods and services.

TODAY'S MONEY IS...
Portable and long-lasting, or durable.
Its value is set – it does not have to be weighed or haggled over.
It can be divided into smaller units, called denominations, so that people can spend a little or a lot and receive change.

☆ WHAT DO WE USE MONEY FOR?

1 AS PAYMENT FOR SERVICES GIVEN

Employees receive a regular sum of money from their employers for work, or labour, carried out.

2 AS A WAY OF GETTING SOMETHING

Some items are necessities, since we need them to survive. Others are luxuries – they are things we would like, but do not actually need. In many societies, people are mainly concerned with satisfying their basic needs, such as food, water and shelter.

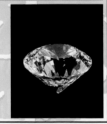

3 AS A WAY OF MAKING AN AGREEMENT

In some societies, the family of the bride gives money, property or other gifts to the bridegroom's family as part of the marriage contract. This payment, or dowry, is particularly common in South Asian countries, such as India and Pakistan.

4 AS A WAY OF SHOWING POWER

Because people value what money can buy, some believe that displaying their wealth makes them appear more powerful.

5

What have been some of the strangest kinds of money used?

Ever since people first traded objects to obtain goods, money has taken on many different forms. Money can be anything at all, as long as its value is recognised and agreed on by everyone using it.

This stone tablet was used in Mesopotamia around 2500 BC, by somebody buying woollen textiles.

☆ COWRIE SHELLS

Around 3,500 years ago shiny, brightly-marked cowrie shells were commonly used as money in China and other parts of Asia, Africa and Australia.

☆ STONE DISCS

The Yap islanders, in the Pacific Ocean, made payments with large stone discs. The biggest discs measured 4m across!

☆ FEATHERS

On the Pacific island of Santa Cruz, a traditional form of payment was a 10m-long coil made from tiny red feathers.

☆ TEA

Blocks, made by pressing together tea and wood shavings, were used as money in China and Tibet until a hundred years ago.

☆ SALT

As part of their wages, Roman soldiers were paid a salarium – an allowance of salt. This is where the word 'salary' comes from.

Connect!

WHAT WILL THE MONEY WE USE IN THE FUTURE BE LIKE? TURN TO Q52.

6

What are coins?

Coins are pieces of metal which represent different amounts of money.

The first coins were made of gold or silver. Today, copper, brass or nickel are used. The two faces of the coin are usually inscribed with pictures and words.

Connect!

TURN TO Q23 TO FIND OUT HOW COINS ARE MADE.

7

When were the first coins made?

The earliest coins are thought to have been made around the 7th century BC.

These coins were made in Lydia, in what is now western Turkey. The bean-shaped lumps were made from electrum – a mixture of gold and silver. Soon, other countries, such as Greece and Italy, started to produce their own coins. By the 5th century BC, coins were common throughout Europe.

8

Can coins be any shape?

Today, most coins are circular, but in the past they came in many shapes and sizes.

BC 500 EARLY CHINESE COINS WERE SHAPED LIKE TOOLS, SUCH AS HOES, SPADES AND KNIVES.	
BC 4 COPPER COINS FROM OLBIA, IN THE USSR, WERE CAST IN THE SHAPE OF A DOLPHIN.	
16TH AND 17TH CENTURIES SQUARE COINS, CALLED KLIPPE, WERE COMMON IN DENMARK.	
1665 THE ENGLISH BRASS PENNY WAS SHAPED LIKE A HEART.	

9 Why do coins have pictures on them?

Connect!

STUDYING THE IMAGES ON COINS HELPS US TO UNDERSTAND HOW PEOPLE LIVED. SEE Q43.

Coins are stamped with words and pictures to show how much they are worth. The designs also show that the coins are genuine and approved by a monarch or government.

⬆ This Greek silver coin, called a tetradrachm, dates from the 5th century BC. It is stamped with an owl, the favourite bird of the goddess Athena.

☆ MINTING THE COINS

A mint is the place where a country's coins are officially made. The process of minting a coin dates back 2,600 years, to Lydian times. A blank piece of metal is stamped with words and pictures, by pressing it between a pair of hard metal surfaces, known as dies. The dies are engraved with the designs for the coin. Early coins showed how much a coin weighed, and featured the image of the monarch to guarantee the weight.

☆ SOUVENIR COINS

Some coins are made to remind people of special events and to celebrate the lives of certain people. These are called commemorative coins.

CHARLES DE GAULLE WAS THE PRESIDENT OF FRANCE FROM 1958 TO 1969. THE 30TH ANNIVERSARY OF HIS ELECTION WAS CELEBRATED IN 1988 WITH A COMMEMORATIVE COIN.

Prove It!

Make a list of the events of the last five years that you would like to see commemorated on a coin. Then choose one and design it.

---

10 Are some coins thought to be lucky?

Some coins were once thought to heal the sick, give protection and bring good fortune.

This Chinese coin shows a figure fighting a demon. A sword made from these coins all tied together was sometimes given to ill people to cure them and to ward off fever demons.

Many German soldiers fighting in the Thirty Years' War (1618-1648) carried coins bearing the image of St George. They believed the coins would protect them from bullets.

---

11 Why do people collect coins?

Coins give us clues about the way people lived and what they believed in.

☆ PEOPLE WHO COLLECT COINS ARE CALLED NUMISMATISTS.

☆ PEOPLE COLLECT COINS BECAUSE...

THEY CAN TEACH US SOMETHING ABOUT THE COUNTRIES THAT ISSUED THEM.	MANY ARE RARE AND VALUABLE. THE HIGHEST PRICE PAID FOR A COIN COLLECTION AT AUCTION IS £11.56 MILLION.	THEY ARE BEAUTIFUL OBJECTS IN THEMSELVES.

QUESTION

12 Who invented paper money?

Paper money was first used in China around the 7th century. Instead of carrying around large amounts of heavy iron coins, people left them with merchants for safe-keeping. In return they received a handwritten receipt. Gradually, people began to trade directly with the receipts as they represented real money.

⬆ This early banknote was made in 1287 in the Mongol empire.

Chinese paper notes often pictured the coins they had been exchanged for. One note could be swapped for hundreds of heavy coins.

Because these pieces of paper were so valuable, they were often quite large. The largest note ever was issued in the 14th century by China's Ming dynasty. It measured 22.8 x 33cm (just bigger than this page) and represented 1,000 coins – which would have weighed about 3.5kg.

⬆ This Chinese note, made in the 14th century, represents 1,000 bronze coins.

Prove It!

This note shows the coins that it represents. If each coin weighs 3g, what total weight of coins does the note represent?

THE ANSWER IS HIDDEN ON THIS PAGE.

Connect!

WHEN DID PEOPLE NEED TO CARRY NOTES AROUND IN BASKETS? SEE Q38.

QUESTION

13 When did paper money change into the banknotes we use today?

It took one thousand years after the Chinese invented paper money before paper notes, representing a value of gold, finally began to be used in Europe.

4

THE FIRST PRINTED NOTES

Britain's Bank of England, set up in 1694, was one of the first banks to issue notes on a regular basis.

1694 THE BANK'S NOTES WERE HANDWRITTEN.
1725 THE £-SIGN AND THE FIRST DIGIT OF THE AMOUNT WAS PRINTED ON THE NOTES.
1745 NOTES WERE PRINTED IN DIFFERENT DENOMINATIONS – FROM £20 TO £1,000.
1855 THE BANK'S FIRST FULLY-PRINTED NOTES APPEARED. THEY WERE THE FORERUNNERS OF THE NOTES IN CIRCULATION AROUND THE WORLD TODAY.

1

THE GOLDSMITHS

In the 16th century, gold was given to goldsmiths, who issued a receipt for it. These 'running cash notes' had the name of the person who had made the deposit written on them. There was also a promise to pay back the money deposited whenever it was demanded.

2

JAPANESE NOTES

Many Japanese temples in the 17th century acted like banks and began to issue their own notes.

3

THE POPE'S NOTES

The 31-scudi note was issued in 1786 by the Bank of the Holy Spirit, in Rome. The bank, set up in 1605 by Pope Paul V, was Europe's first national bank.

Connect!

HOW ARE BANKNOTES MADE TODAY? FIND OUT IN Q24.

14

Why do notes look like they do?

Banknotes are designed to be pleasing to the eye, easily recognisable, difficult to forge and cheap to produce. The notes may feature people and events that are important to the country issuing them.

☆ THE SIZE

In many countries, the more valuable the note is, the larger it is.

☆ THE COLOUR

To avoid confusion, denominations of notes are usually given their own unique colour.

☆ **THE EXCEPTION** IN THE USA, THE 1, 2, 5, 10, 20, 50 AND 100 DOLLAR NOTES ARE ALL THE SAME SIZE (ABOUT 15.6 X 6.6CM) AND COLOUR (BLACK INK IS USED ON THE FRONT AND GREEN ON THE BACK).

☆ THE PICTURES

Examining notes can tell us much about the history of the country that issued them.

☆ BANKNOTES FROM KAMPUCHEA, IN SOUTH-EAST ASIA, OFTEN SHOW SCENES DEPICTING THE COUNTRY'S CHIEF INDUSTRIES, SUCH AS AGRICULTURE AND FISHING.

☆ THE FRENCH 100-FRANC NOTE FEATURES THE ARTIST EUGÈNE DELACROIX (1798-1863) AND PART OF HIS REVOLUTIONARY PAINTING *LIBERTY LEADING THE PEOPLE.*

Prove It!

Look closely at this banknote. Where does it come from and how much is it worth?

THE ANSWER IS HIDDEN ON THIS PAGE.

Connect!

HOW DO BANKS MAKE BANKNOTES DIFFICULT TO COPY? SEE Q28.

15

Are all notes used to buy things?

No. Some notes are thought to have special meanings. They may be used as part of religious festivals, or artists may use them to make a statement about the way we live.

Connect!

FIND OUT HOW BANKNOTES ARE DESTROYED IN Q16.

PEOPLE TRY TO MAKE THEIR WISHES COME TRUE BY THROWING COINS INTO A WISHING WELL.

☆ BURNING NOTES AS PART OF A FESTIVAL

The Chinese print special imitation banknotes, known as hell money. Each

bears a value of many millions of dollars. People burn hell money during the month-long Festival of Ghosts, for their ancestors to use in the spirit world.

☆ BURNING NOTES TO MAKE A POINT

In November 1994, Bill Drummond and Jimmy Cauty, of the British pop group KLF, withdrew £1 million from their bank accounts. They then flew to a small Scottish island and set fire to the money inside a shed. Cauty explained afterwards: "It was to do with us controlling the money, and not the money controlling us."

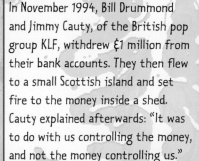

☆ PROVE IT1 ANSWER: GERMANY, 100 MARKS.

16 Why is money withdrawn from use?

Every day millions of banknotes and coins are destroyed. This may be because they have become dirty, torn or just worn-out. It may even be because the notes and coins are fakes, or forgeries.

Connect!

CHECK OUT Q28 TO FIND OUT MORE ABOUT FORGERY.

☆ HOW LONG DOES MONEY LAST?

● Coins can be used for 20 to 30 years before the image wears away. Some coins may also be withdrawn from circulation if the government no longer wishes them to be currency.

● Paper money is more fragile. Low denomination notes pass from one person to another so rapidly that they may only last a few months. Higher value notes can last for three to four years.

☆ HOW IS MONEY DESTROYED?

Banks return used notes to a central bank, which controls the amount of money in circulation. Here, special sorting machines separate the money out into three main piles:

NOTES WHICH ARE IN FINE CONDITION = RE-ISSUED FOR FURTHER CIRCULATION.	NOTES WHICH ARE FAKES, OR FORGERIES = DESTROYED.	NOTES WHICH ARE WORN, BADLY SOILED OR TORN = DESTROYED.

Notes are destroyed by being shredded into 1mm squares. Or they may be burnt in an incinerator and the ash ground up to make sure that no trace of the money remains (right).

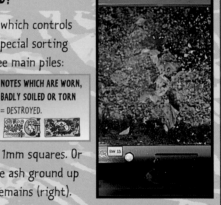

Connect!

TURN TO Q30 TO READ ABOUT A FAMOUS ROBBERY THAT INTERCEPTED THE MONEY ON ITS WAY TO BEING DESTROYED.

17 Why does money come in different values?

THE HIGHEST VALUE BANKNOTES IN CIRCULATION ARE US FEDERAL RESERVE $10,000 NOTES. CURRENTLY THERE ARE 345 OF THE NOTES IN CIRCULATION.

The first banknotes represented the exact sum of money deposited in the bank by the customer. But in the 18th century, banks started to fix the amounts shown on the notes. This was convenient for the banks and for the people exchanging the notes for goods and services.

↑ Portugal's coin denominations are 1, 2.5, 5, 10, 20, 25, 50, 100 and 200 escudo.

Prove It!

Imagine a banknote worth ₤1 million. Why do you think banknotes with such a large denomination are not used on a day-to-day basis?

☆ AUSTRALIAN BANKNOTES ARE PRINTED ON PLASTIC, WHICH MAKES THEM LAST LONGER AND MORE DIFFICULT TO FORGE.

☆ IN THE PAST, BANKS USED NOTES INTERNALLY REPRESENTING ₤1 MILLION, TO HELP THEM CALCULATE HOW MUCH MONEY THEY HAD.

Why is gold valuable?

Gold was one of the first metals that people discovered and used. Throughout the ages, owning gold has been a sign of wealth. It is valuable because it is scarce and also beautiful. When gold takes the form of coins or bars, it is a good way of storing money.

IT TAKES 100 TONNES OF GOLD-BEARING ROCK TO PRODUCE JUST 1KG OF GOLD.

⬆ Gold bars are used by countries as a form of money to make payment to each other. Until the 1930s, most countries followed the gold standard – a system where a country's currency could be exchanged for a fixed weight of gold.

☆ GOLD RUSH

A gold rush is a large, rapid movement of people to an area where gold has been found.

● MID-19TH CENTURY
Large amounts of gold were discovered in parts of the USA, South Africa, Australia and New Zealand. Towns grew overnight as people from all over the world flocked to claim a piece of land.

● 1996
A modern-day gold rush was triggered in northern Ontario, Canada, when rich deposits of gold and other metals were found.

☆ THE MIDAS TOUCH

'Having the Midas touch' means that any project you turn your hand to ends up making money. King Midas was a character in an ancient Greek story, who had the power to turn everything he touched into gold.

Prove It!

Gold is very versatile. How many things made of gold can you name? How many words or phrases containing 'gold' can you think of?

Connect!

GOLD HAS FEATURED IN MANY STORIES AND FILMS. SEE Q51.

What is a bank?

A bank is a place where people can store their money. A bank also lends money to people who need it – this may be an individual, a business and even a government.

☆ THE FIRST BANKS

Banking, as we know it today, developed between the 13th and 17th centuries in Italy. The word 'bank' comes from the Italian 'banco', meaning bench. Moneylenders sat on benches in the marketplace, waiting to do business.

☆ HOW DOES A BANK WORK?

THIS PERSON STORES, OR DEPOSITS, SOME MONEY IN THE BANK. THEY ARE LENDING FUNDS TO THE BANK.

IN RETURN, THE BANK REGULARLY PAYS THE PERSON INTEREST – AN AMOUNT OF MONEY IN ADDITION TO THE ORIGINAL SUM DEPOSITED.

THIS PERSON NEEDS MONEY. HE GOES TO THE BANK TO ASK FOR A LOAN.

THE PERSON BORROWING THE MONEY MUST PAY BACK EXTRA MONEY AT REGULAR INTERVALS, IN ADDITION TO THE ORIGINAL SUM BORROWED. THIS IS ALSO CALLED INTEREST.

A BANK LENDS MONEY DEPOSITED BY ONE BORROWER TO OTHER BORROWERS AND COLLECTS INTEREST ON THE LOANS. THIS IS USED TO PAY THE BANK'S EXPENSES AND TO AWARD INTEREST TO ITS DEPOSITORS.

QUESTION

20 What is a cheque?

A cheque is a written instruction to a bank to pay a sum of money from your bank account either to yourself or to another person. The person receiving the money is called the 'payee'.

ALTHOUGH MOST CHEQUES TAKE THE FORM OF SPECIALLY PRINTED SLIPS, THEY CAN ACTUALLY BE WRITTEN ON ANYTHING AT ALL. PEOPLE HAVE PAID BILLS WITH CHEQUES WRITTEN ON BANANAS, PAVING STONES AND EVEN COWS!

☆ GUARANTEEING THE CHEQUE

In some countries, a cheque cannot be used without a cheque guarantee card. As well as acting as a form of identification, the card promises to pay out the money written on the cheque up to a certain amount — even if there is not enough money in the account to cover it.

Traveller's cheques

These cheques are bought from a bank or travel agent and are used by people going on holiday. Once in a foreign country, they can be exchanged for the local currency. They are safer than carrying money because they can be replaced if lost.

QUESTION

21 What is 'plastic money'?

Many types of plastic cards can be used instead of cash. They work by transferring money between accounts.

☆ PLASTIC

● People use credit and charge cards to buy goods and services and pay for them later. The company issuing the card pays the shop for your purchase and sends you the bill. You must pay within a certain time otherwise interest is charged on the original amount spent.

● Phonecards can be used in many public telephones instead of coins. The value of the card is stored on a magnetic coating on the back. The cost of a call is automatically deducted each time the card is used.

⬆ This is an automatic teller machine (ATM). It is operated by a cash card and lets you withdraw money from your bank account at any time. There is usually a limit to how much money you can take out. An ATM may also accept deposits and tell you how much money you have in your account.

QUESTION

22 Can money become more important than what it can buy?

Yes. Some people value the coins and notes themselves more than what they can buy. We call these people misers.

The greatest ever miser may have been an American lady called Henrietta Green. She had $95 million, but chose to eat cold porridge rather than spend money on heating it up!

☆ IN *A CHRISTMAS CAROL*, THE AUTHOR CHARLES DICKENS (1812–70) WROTE ABOUT A MISER CALLED EBENEZER SCROOGE. THIS MAN REFUSED TO SPEND ANY MONEY ON HIMSELF, OR ANYONE ELSE, UNTIL THREE GHOSTS SHOWED HIM THE ERROR OF HIS GREEDY WAYS!

Connect!
HOW WILL WE USE MONEY IN THE FUTURE? SEE Q52.

Connect!
HOW DO PEOPLE BECOME MILLIONAIRES? FIND OUT IN Q32.

Let's take a look at

making money

How are banknotes made?

How do we protect money?

What is forgery?

If you want to find out the answers to all these questions and many more, just turn the page and move on to PART TWO of your journey. ---→

QUESTION

23 How are coins made?

Coins have been made in the same basic way for 2,600 years: an image is stamped onto a piece of metal by pressing it between two hard metal surfaces. In the past, the process was carried out by hand, but today electrically-powered machines are used.

Prove It!

Make your own die. Use a spoon to gouge out a simple design into a halved potato. Then push this potato die firmly into modelling clay – and pull away to reveal your raised design in the clay!

1 MAKING A MODEL OF THE COIN

An artist creates a model made from plaster. They use metal tools to make the design as detailed as possible. This model is much larger than the finished coin.

2 MAKING A METAL MODEL

A metal version, made of nickel, is produced from the plaster model using a complicated process known as electrotyping.

3 REDUCING THE SIZE OF THE MODEL

A machine known as a reducing lathe traces the lines on the electrotype model and carves them in miniature on a piece of steel, called a hub (or punch). The hub is the same size as the actual coin.

4 MAKING THE DIE

The hub is strengthened with heat and chemicals, and used to make a coin-stamping die.

5 MAKING THE FINAL COIN

Two dies – one for each side of the coin – are fitted to a high speed press. Plain pieces of metal, known as blanks, are fed into the press, where they are squashed between the dies. The image on the dies is stamped onto the blanks – and a new batch of coins is minted!

QUESTION

24 How are banknotes made?

Banknotes are made by using sophisticated technology and complicated methods, in order to make the notes as difficult to copy as possible.

Many central banks produce the banknotes for a country, and usually have their own printing works. The Bureau of Engraving and Printing, Washington DC, designs and prints the USA's paper currency – about 23 million notes a day!

1 THE DESIGN

An artist produces sketches of the note. These are traditionally done in pencil and ink, but computer-aided design (CAD) is used to draw the intricate, geometric patterns for the background.

2 MAKING PLATES

An engraver uses sharp tools to etch the image by hand, back-to-front, into a steel intaglio plate. The design is copied many times onto a large printing plate. This prints a whole sheet of notes.

25

Who decides what money looks like?

Ever since coins and notes were first used, the look of money has largely been decided by the government of a country. But individuals can sometimes have their say too.

An artist draws sketches for a new note or coin, detailing all the pictures and colours to be used. The designs are then shown to the government's treasury department. This looks after the country's money, and needs to approve any new designs before production can begin.

NOT ALL DESIGNS ARE POPULAR WITH THE PUBLIC. A CANADIAN $1 NOTE ISSUED IN 1954 FEATURED A PORTRAIT OF QUEEN ELIZABETH II. BUT THE QUEEN'S HAIR WAS DRAWN IN SUCH A WAY THAT A DEVIL'S FACE SEEMED TO APPEAR IN IT. PEOPLE REFUSED TO USE THE NOTES, AND THEY WERE EVENTUALLY WITHDRAWN.

Victory

In the 3rd century BC, the Roman armies conquered much of the land around the western Mediterranean. They insisted that the people used coins showing pictures of their victories. They also prevented cities in Italy and Sicily from minting their own coins.

War

In 1931, the Japanese armies invaded China (below). They set up new banks and issued their own money.

Peace

In 1973, a special 50-pence coin was made as a souvenir of Britain joining the European Economic Community (EEC), an organisation encouraging trade between member countries. The linked hands are meant to reflect unity between EEC members.

Connect! FIND OUT HOW MONEY IS USED IN WAR IN Q42.

☆ EURO MONEY

A challenge was set to design the notes for a single European currency, called the euro. To gauge public opinion, the ten best ideas were shown to 2,000 people. The final decision was taken by the European Monetary Institute, which acts like a central bank for the whole of Europe.

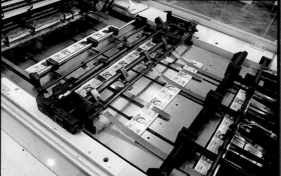

3 MIXING THE INK

The inks have to be combined very carefully, in order to create the exact colours for the notes.

4 MAKING THE PAPER

Banknotes are handled by many people, so they need to be hard-wearing. They are usually printed on paper made from cotton fibre and linen rag, rather than weaker wood pulp.

5 PRINTING

The sheets of notes are printed using three main processes:

● **OFFSET LITHOGRAPHY:** PRINTS THE BACKGROUND DESIGN. Lithography plates are made from the intaglio plate. Each carries a different colour. Ink is transfered from rollers onto the plates and then onto the paper. Each plate has a different colour. These are printed on top of each other.
● **INTAGLIO:** PRODUCES THE MAIN IMAGE ON THE NOTE. The ink is forced out of the grooves on the plate and onto the paper.
● **LETTERPRESS:** PRINTS A UNIQUE SERIAL NUMBER ON EACH NOTE. But, before the numbers are added, the notes are checked for any flaws.

6 BUNDLING AND DELIVERING

Finally, a guillotine cuts the sheets of notes into individual notes. They are then packed into bundles, shrinkwrapped and delivered to the banks.

Connect! WHAT IS SPECIAL ABOUT THE PRINTERS WHO MAKE BANKNOTES? SEE Q26.

QUESTION 26

What's special about the printers who make banknotes?

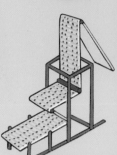

Notes are mass-produced, which means large quantities are made at the same time. To be able to cope, banknote printers need to have fast and accurate printing presses. They must also be able to incorporate security features, such as serial numbers and metallic strips, into the notes.

☆ KEEPING A SECRET

Only a few printers are asked to print banknotes. The government of a country trusts the company to keep the printing process confidential and to destroy any notes that are not perfect.

↑ An intaglio printing press used to print money at De La Rue.

The printer

NAME: De La Rue
BASED: London, England.
BUSINESS: De La Rue is the world's largest currency printer. It produces notes for about two-thirds of the available international market, including many of the newly-formed states in eastern Europe. It constantly experiments with new security features to try to protect notes from forgery. Specimens showing the company's latest ideas are sent to banks all over the world.

↑ This De La Rue 'house note' is used by the company to test that their security features work.

QUESTION 27

How do we protect money?

Most people keep their money safe by depositing it in a bank. All the cash is stored in strong, fireproof vaults, making it almost impossible to steal. If any money does get stolen, the bank is insured against theft – which means an insurance company will replace the missing amount.

Connect!

CAN A BANK EVER RUN OUT OF MONEY? TO FIND OUT TURN TO Q39.

BEFORE BANKS, PEOPLE HAD TO DECIDE HOW TO LOOK AFTER THEIR MONEY...

1 THEY COULD GIVE IT TO A GOLDSMITH

They could give their money to a merchant or a goldsmith. They would receive a hand-written receipt in exchange.

2 THEY COULD CARRY THE CASH

They could carry the money around with them, in a purse or wallet. But this meant possibly losing it or even having it stolen.

● IN THE EARLY 18TH CENTURY, GOLD AND SILVER COINS WERE CARRIED AROUND IN POUCH-LIKE LEATHER PURSES.

28 What is forgery?

A piece of metal or paper only has the value of money if it is genuine. It must be made in a specific way and issued by the correct authority. People who copy the real thing are committing the crime of forgery.

Prove It!

Which banknote is genuine and which is a forgery? THE ANSWER IS HIDDEN ON THIS PAGE.

1

2

☆ CRIME AND PUNISHMENT

● Because money is usually issued by a monarch or a government, tampering with coins and notes, or making your own without authorisation, is a crime against the state.

● Making false, or counterfeit, money is a serious offence. In the past, forgers had their hands chopped off or were executed. Today, they face heavy fines or imprisonment.

☆ THE METHODS

PLATING THE COINS
INSTEAD OF USING SOLID GOLD, A PIECE OF CHEAP METAL, SUCH AS COPPER, COULD BE COVERED IN A GOLD PLATING. THE PLATING WOULD FEATURE THE DESIGN OF THE REAL COINS. THIS ANCIENT GREEK COIN WAS CUT TO MAKE SURE THAT IT WAS SOLID SILVER AND NOT A FORGERY.

COPYING THE NOTE
BEFORE THE INVENTION OF COPYING MACHINES, MANY FORGERS WOULD SPEND A GREAT DEAL OF TIME AND EFFORT COPYING EVERY DETAIL OF A NOTE BY HAND.

INVENTING A BANK
IN THE 1970s, ITALIAN SHOPKEEPERS RAN OUT OF SMALL CHANGE, SO THEY GAVE OUT TELEPHONE TOKENS AND SWEETS INSTEAD. BANKS STARTED TO ISSUE SMALL-CHANGE NOTES. ONE FORGER TOOK ADVANTAGE OF THE SITUATION AND ISSUED NOTES IN THE NAME OF A BANK THAT DIDN'T EVEN EXIST!

☆ FIGHTING THE FORGERS

ANTI-FORGERY FEATURES ON BANKNOTES INCLUDE:
● WATERMARK = A PICTURE THAT CAN BE ONLY BE SEEN WHEN THE NOTE IS HELD UP TO THE LIGHT.
● SECURITY THREAD = A METALLIC THREAD EMBEDDED WITHIN THE PAPER.
● SERIAL NUMBER = A NUMBER WHICH ALLOWS NOTES TO BE TRACKED.
● COMPLEX GEOMETRICAL PATTERNS = THESE MAY ONLY BECOME CLEAR IF BOTH SIDES OF THE NOTE ARE PRINTED EXACTLY.
● PASTEL COLOURS = THESE ARE DIFFICULT TO PHOTOCOPY ACCURATELY.
● METAL FOILS = THESE TURN BLACK ON PHOTOCOPIES.

⬆ The world's biggest gold reserves are in America. Fort Knox, in Kentucky, alone holds around $40,000 million of gold bars, or bullion. With its high-tech security measures, bomb-proof vaults and 24-hour patrols by armed guards, Fort Knox is impossible to break into.

Prove It!

You have been given some money to look after. How will you protect it? Match the options to the outcome of your choices. THE ANSWERS ARE HIDDEN ON THIS PAGE.

THE OPTIONS

1 ☆ GIVE IT TO A BANK.

2 ☆ CARRY IT IN YOUR POCKETS.

3 ☆ PUT IT IN A PIGGY BANK.

4 ☆ BURY IT.

THE OUTCOME

A YOU MIGHT FORGET WHERE YOU HID IT.

B YOU'LL SAVE THE MONEY – BUT NOT EARN ANY INTEREST.

C YOU MIGHT LOSE IT, OR BE TEMPTED TO SPEND IT.

D YOU'LL SAVE THE MONEY – AND EARN INTEREST ON IT.

Connect!

THE PIRATES STOLE TREASURE – BUT WHO DID IT BELONG TO? SEE Q29.

IN THE 19TH CENTURY, [PEO]PLE USED ORNATE DRESS [PUR]SES, WHICH WERE [ATT]ACHED TO THEIR BELTS.

● TODAY, SOME PEOPLE WEAR MONEY BELTS WITH ZIPPED COMPARTMENTS TO PREVENT PICKPOCKETS FROM STEALING THE CONTENTS.

3 THEY COULD KEEP IT IN A MONEY BOX

With most metal money boxes, it was impossible to get hold of the money inside without a key.

● THE EARLIEST KNOWN 'PIGGY BANKS' WERE USED IN INDONESIA IN THE 14TH CENTURY. TO GET THE MONEY OUT, THE POTTERY PIGS HAD TO BE SMASHED!

4 THEY COULD BURY IT

Many people hid their money by burying it. Money that was not recovered was sometimes discovered years later by accident. Such finds are called treasure-trove. In some countries, whoever finds the treasure-trove can keep some, or all, of it. In others, it belongs by law to the king or queen. The finder is given some money as a reward.

QUESTION

29

What is a pirate and who do they steal from?

The word 'pirate' comes from the Greek 'peiran', meaning 'to attack'. Pirates are people who rob ships at sea. They are also known as buccaneers or pickaroons.

☝ Pirate ships often flew the Jolly Roger – a black-and-white flag showing a skull and crossbones.

☆ WHY BECOME A PIRATE?

● Life at sea was so harsh that seamen on trade ships sometimes seized control of their vessels. This was called mutiny.
● Piracy gave people a chance to become rich quickly. It also gave them a feeling of power.
● Many sailors became pirates when they were no longer needed to fight for their countries.

Treasure

By the middle of the 16th century, Spain controlled most of South America. Gold and silver found in Mexico and Peru was made into coins – silver 'pieces of eight' (a Spanish coin worth eight reales) and gold doubloons. Loaded onto ships bound for Europe, the cargo was a prime target for pirates!

☆ PIRATES TODAY

The world's navies have wiped out most piracy. But pirates still roam the South China Sea, the coasts of west Africa and Brazil, and the Caribbean. They prey on slow-moving tankers and freighters. Instead of cutlasses, today's pirates are armed with grenades and machine guns.

QUESTION

30

Can people become famous for robbery?

Stealing money can bring the robber notoriety as well as wealth. Tales of daring robberies are common.

Connect!

HOW DOES POWER BRING YOU MONEY? FIND OUT IN Q42.

☆ HIGH-TECH CRIME

A hacker is someone who secretly uses, or changes, the information in other people's computer systems. Hackers can gain access to a company's computers via a telephone line – they then crack the security passwords and steal the data. In the US, hacking costs businesses an estimated $150 billion a year.

☆ THE GREAT TRAIN ROBBERY

On 8 August 1963, a gang of robbers stole £2.6 million in used banknotes from a British mail train. The money was on its way from Glasgow to London to be destroyed. People were so fascinated by this story that a film was made of it in 1988. It is called *Buster* (above).

☆ ROBBING FROM THE RICH...

ROBIN HOOD AND HIS BAND OF FOLLOWERS, OR MERRY MEN, WERE LEGENDARY ENGLISH OUTLAWS. THEY ARE SAID TO HAVE LIVED IN SHERWOOD FOREST, NOTTINGHAMSHIRE, DURING THE 12TH CENTURY. STORIES TELL OF HOW THEY STOLE FROM THE RICH TO GIVE TO THE POOR.

HIGHWAYMEN TERRORISED WEALTHY ROAD TRAVELLERS DURING THE 17TH AND 18TH CENTURIES. DRESSED IN CLOAKS AND MASKS, THEY WOULD HOLD UP CARRIAGES WITH PISTOLS. FRENCHMAN CLAUDE DUVAL WAS A FAMOUS HIGHWAYMAN OF THE LATE 1600s.

☆ COMPUTER HACKER PHIBER OPTIK (REAL NAME MARK ABENE) HIT THE HEADLINES IN THE EARLY 1990s. NEWSPAPERS AND MAGAZINES ALL OVER THE WORLD INTERVIEWED HIM. HE EVEN APPEARED ON TELEVISION GIVING DEMONSTRATIONS OF HIS HACKING SKILLS. HIS CELEBRITY STATUS ENDED IN 1993, WHEN HE WAS ARRESTED AND SENT TO JAIL.

Connect!

HOW DO RICH COUNTRIES TRY TO HELP POOR COUNTRIES TODAY? SEE Q41.

Money and the

world

How do rich countries help poor countries?

Can money become worthless?

How do people become millionaires?

To find out how money affects the
way we live, turn the page and move
on to PART THREE ---➤

QUESTION

31 How do people earn money?

People earn money for work that they have done. Some people are given money as a gift. People become wealthy if they can earn much more money than they spend on the goods and services they need or want.

WHAT IS A PERSON'S INCOME?

→ YOUR INCOME IS THE TOTAL AMOUNT OF MONEY YOU RECEIVE...

☆ MONEY FROM WORK

WAGE THIS IS THE MONEY THAT AN EMPLOYER PAYS A PERSON WORKING FOR THEM (AN EMPLOYEE). WAGES ARE USUALLY PAID DAILY, WEEKLY OR MONTHLY, IN THE FORM OF CASH OR CHEQUES. THE AMOUNT RECEIVED DEPENDS ON THE NUMBER OF HOURS WORKED OR THE QUANTITY OF GOODS PRODUCED.

SALARY AGAIN, THIS IS A SUM OF MONEY PAID BY AN EMPLOYER TO AN EMPLOYEE. SALARY IS USUALLY PAID DIRECTLY INTO THE EMPLOYEE'S BANK ACCOUNT ONCE A WEEK OR MONTH. THE AMOUNT OF THE SALARY IS FIXED.

☆ MONEY FROM SAVINGS AND GIFTS

INTEREST FROM SAVINGS A person may deposit money in a bank, which will keep it safe and earn them interest. This interest is called profit, as it is money gained.

MONEY AS A GIFT A person may receive money on a special occasion, such as a birthday. When someone dies, they may pass any money they have to relatives.

MONEY FROM OTHER AREAS A person may make money by renting out property, or by buying goods cheaply and selling them on at a higher price.

INCOME

☆ THE LARGEST EVER SINGLE CASH GIFT WAS GIVEN TO MORE THAN 4,000 US SCHOOLS BY THE FORD FOUNDATION IN 1955. AT THE TIME, IT WAS WORTH $180 MILLION.

Connect! DO SOME PEOPLE GIVE MONEY AWAY? FIND OUT IN Q34.

Prove It!

A person may spend money on objects of value – such as a house, a car or a painting. These are called assets. You have $50,000. What will you spend it on?

☆ **A HOUSE** Once purchased, the house will need to be maintained and the bills paid regularly. If you want to sell it in the future, it may be worth more money than the price you originally paid for it.

☆ **A CAR** You need to make regular payments for petrol, oil and insurance. Carrying out repairs costs money. A classic car is one that is old or rare – or both. It often becomes more valuable with age.

☆ **A PAINTING** Having bought the painting, there are few extra costs. You may want to insure it. A painting by a famous artist, especially if they are no longer alive, may increase in value.

Why do some people earn more than others?

THE MONEY THAT YOU EARN FOR THE WORK THAT YOU DO DEPENDS ON...

HOW MUCH MONEY AN EMPLOYER CAN AFFORD TO SPEND.

HOW IMPORTANT IT IS THAT *YOU* ARE DOING THE JOB.

HOW VALUABLE YOUR WORK IS TO YOUR EMPLOYER.

HOW MUCH MONEY AN EMPLOYER MAKES OUT OF THE WORK YOU DO.

HOW MANY PEOPLE COULD DO YOUR JOB.

HOW MANY PEOPLE WOULD WANT TO DO YOUR JOB.

⬆ These workers are assembling microwave ovens on a production line. Although the work requires some skill they may not earn much money for their labour.

⬆ This surgeon has a highly specialised job. He is paid a large salary, because few people could do his job without years of education and training.

32

How do people become millionaires?

Connect!

FIND OUT HOW SHARES ARE BOUGHT AND SOLD IN Q48.

Some people have a talent or skill that is thought to be valuable. They may be given large amounts of money for the work they do. Others own, or invest in, something that is worth a great deal. People who have money can use that money to make more money.

1 Money makes money

SHARES By buying shares in a company, a person can claim a part of the company's profits. Shareholders receive this payment in the form of dividends.

BUSINESS Running a successful business can make people very wealthy indeed. The Microsoft Corporation was set up in 1975. Today, it is the world's largest software company and its chairman and co-founder, Bill Gates, is a multi-billionaire.

BANKS The larger the sum of money deposited in a bank, the more interest it gains. If the interest paid on £1 million is £126 a day, then the interest paid on £1 billion is £126,000.

2 Owning something valuable

People in Saudi Arabia used to be very poor, surviving by subsistence farming – growing just enough food to feed themselves and their families. Fortunes changed with the discovery, beneath the desert, of the biggest known oil reserves in the world. Today, millions of barrels of oil are sold to countries around the globe. The Saudis are now the richest group of people in the Middle East.

Connect!

HOW ELSE CAN MONEY MAKE MONEY? TURN TO Q33.

Prove It!

You can earn a lot of interest on a large enough deposit. Suppose a bank pays an annual interest of 4%. How much interest will you earn on £10 and £5,000? To work out the answers, multiply each amount by 4 and divide by 100.

THE ANSWERS ARE HIDDEN ON THIS PAGE.

3 Paying for the person

People who entertain the world, such as musicians, singers, actors and sports stars, can become very rich indeed. The general public decides how valuable an individual is, by choosing to support one person above another. If a person attracts fans to their film or show, or sells many records, their management companies will give them more money for their next project.

THE SINGER
NAME: **MADONNA**
REASON FOR WEALTH: She has recorded more than 50 hit songs and starred in concerts and films. She has a personal fortune of around $350 million.

THE ACTOR
NAME: **ARNOLD SCHWARZENEGGER**
REASON FOR WEALTH: He has starred in more than 30 successful films. He earns around $25 million per film.

THE SPORTSMAN
NAME: **MICHAEL JORDAN**
REASON FOR WEALTH: As well as being a top basketball player, he stars in films and endorses companies' products. He is worth about $100 million.

⬆ Some individuals are very wealthy indeed. One of the richest people in the world is the Sultan of Brunei. He has an estimated fortune of around £27 billion.

☆ PROVE IT! ANSWERS: 40p; £200.

33 What is gambling?

People who gamble bet money on the outcome of a game, event or chance happening. If they predict correctly they may win a great deal of money. Most gambles don't pay off, and the gambler can go broke.

Prove It!

When you toss a coin, there is an equal chance of it landing on either side. Flip a coin 20 times and with each turn try to predict on which side it will land. If you had bet money on each outcome, would you have made a profit or a loss by the end?

☆ WHY GAMBLE?

PEOPLE GAMBLE BECAUSE...
● They get a thrill from taking risks – it makes them feel adventurous.
● They enjoy competing against others.
● It can be a quick way to make a lot of money.
● They feel the excitement of winning is worth the disappointment of losing.

THE ROMANS ENJOYED GAMBLING – THEY LAID BETS ON SPECTACULAR CHARIOT RACES.

Casinos

Casinos are buildings where people go to try to win money by gambling. They may play card games, such as poker, dice games, such as craps, and roulette, where players try to guess in which square on a spinning wheel they think a ball will drop.

⬆ The Mediterranean town of Monte Carlo, Monaco, has been famous as a gambling resort since the middle of the 19th century. Wealthy players come from all over the world.

In a casino, players usually buy and play with plastic coins, called chips. These are a form of money that can only be used inside the casino. At the end of a game, the chips are exchanged for cash. This casino chip represents one dollar.

☆ OTHER WAYS TO WIN OR LOSE

LOTTERIES
People buy a lottery ticket and choose several numbers. The winner is the person whose numbers match those picked at random by a computer.

SLOT MACHINES
People feed coins into the machine and pull a lever on its side. This sets a group of reels spinning. You win money depending on the sequence of pictures shown on the reels when they stop.

☆ THE BIGGEST EVER GAMBLING WIN WAS IN JULY 1993, BY A COUPLE FROM WISCONSIN, USA. THEY WON $111,240,463.10 IN A LOTTERY GAME.

34 Do some people give their money away?

Many people give money to charities. Others make donations to events and places.

Prove It!

Imagine a world without possessions. Imagine owning just the clothes on your back, eating very simple food and living in just one room. How would you feel?

☆ GIVING UP MONEY

SOME PEOPLE LIVE A LIFE FREE FROM HAVING TO MAKE CHOICES ABOUT WHAT TO SPEND MONEY ON. CHRISTIAN MONKS AND NUNS OBSERVE A VOW OF POVERTY. THIS MEANS THAT THEY CANNOT OWN ANY PRIVATE POSSESSIONS OR MONEY. ALL THEIR NEEDS ARE TAKEN CARE OF BY THE MONASTERY OR NUNNERY.

☆ GIVING OUT MONEY

SOME PEOPLE HAVE SO MUCH MONEY THAT THEY CAN AFFORD TO DONATE A PART OF IT TO OTHER PEOPLE, OR TO PLACES OR WORTHY CAUSES. BRITISH BUSINESSMAN GEORGE SOROS HAS AN ANNUAL INCOME OF £650 MILLION. OF THIS, HE DONATES AROUND £100 MILLION EACH YEAR TO CAUSES IN EASTERN EUROPE. HE SAYS: "I WANT TO FURTHER THOSE SOCIETIES WHERE A PERSON OF ANY RACE CAN LIVE IN PEACE."

Connect!

WHY ARE PEOPLE IN SOME COUNTRIES VERY POOR? SEE Q40.

☆ A CHARITY IS AN ORGANISATION THAT RELIES ON DONATIONS FROM INDIVIDUALS. MANY CHARITIES EXIST TO HELP PEOPLE IN NEED.

35 What does it mean to become bankrupt?

When a person or business does not have enough money to pay their debts, they declare themselves bankrupt. Their assets – equipment or property of value – are sold and the money raised divided up between the people who are owed money.

The word 'bankrupt' comes from an Italian word meaning 'broken bench'. In 16th century Italy, moneylenders whose businesses failed had their benches broken. It was a sign to other people that the business had collapsed.

☆ IN THE PAST

In ancient Rome, people who could not pay their debts had their possessions taken from them. These were then handed over to those people who were owed money.

☆ GETTING INTO TROUBLE

In Japan, moneylenders known as the Sarakin charge such a high rate of interest that most people stand little chance of ever settling a loan. Some Sarakin companies hire gangsters to force people into paying up. Many people run away from their homes to try and escape the Sarakin.

NAME: M C HAMMER
CLAIM TO FAME: This American rap star had many hit records in the early 1990s.
THEN: He earned around $30 million each year. He bought a multi-million dollar mansion, a private jet, 17 cars, his own record label, racehorses and even a gold-plated lavatory!
NOW: His spending took its toll. In 1996, M C Hammer was bankrupt, with debts of almost $14 million.

---

36 What is the cost of living?

The cost of living is the amount of money that people have to pay for goods and services in the country they live in.

☆ LIVING STANDARDS

A person's living standard is the difference between the amount they earn and the amount they pay out. The amount of money people pay for things (the cost of living) varies around the world. The amount of money they earn (income) also varies. So the same sum of money in one country may buy more, or less, goods in a different country.

☆ EARNING AND BUYING

COUNTRY	AVERAGE INCOME (IN US $)	COST OF A CANNED DRINK (IN US $)
DENMARK	$24,960	$2
USA	$23,750	75 CENTS
UK	$16,920	60 CENTS
AUSTRALIA	$16,630	$1
INDIA	$350	15 CENTS

---

37 What is inflation?

Inflation is the increase in prices over a period of time. This increase may be small (creeping inflation) or very large (hyperinflation). Inflation decreases the value of money.

☆ LESS FOR YOUR MONEY

If prices rise, people cannot buy as much with their money and their living standards fall. The wage increases they may demand push up the cost of producing goods, which in turn pushes up prices. Inflation affects everyone, but hits the poor the hardest. As the cost of essential goods and services increases, their small incomes pay for less and less.

HYPERINFLATION IN SOUTH AMERICA

BRAZIL

BOLIVIA

IN THE 1980S, IN BOLIVIA, THE PRICE OF FLOUR ROSE BY 50,500%. THE PRICE OF COOKING OIL ROSE BY 111,458%.

☆ MOST COUNTRIES AIM TO KEEP THE INFLATION RATE BETWEEN 3% AND 5%. THIS MEANS PRICES REMAIN RELATIVELY STABLE.

38

Can money become worthless?

Yes! The value of money depends on what you can buy with it. Money becomes worthless when prices are so high that the cash you have buys you nothing at all. Another way that money loses its value is if coins and notes are withdrawn from circulation, as they can no longer be exchanged for goods or services.

Prove It!

How would you deal with hyperinflation? The German people bartered cigarettes, coffee and sugar with each other. Imagine if a book you wanted became 1,000 times more expensive overnight. What would you do?

1 ☆ DECIDE TO DO WITHOUT IT?

2 ☆ SAVE UP UNTIL YOU COULD AFFORD IT?

3 ☆ SELL WHAT YOU HAD AND USE THE MONEY TO BUY THE BOOK?

1 — ACCEPTED BY ALL

Money only has a value if it is accepted in exchange for whatever you want to spend it on.

In 1271, the Italian explorer Marco Polo visited Kublai Khan – the Mongol leader who had taken over China. He found that Khan was printing his own money and paying the Mongol soldiers with it. When Khan's armies were thrown out of China in 1358, their paper money became unacceptable and worthless.

2 — OUT OF CIRCULATION

In 1971, Britain's centuries-old currency (which had 12 pennies to a shilling and 20 shillings to a pound) was withdrawn from circulation. It was replaced by a decimal currency (where money is divided into units of 10). This made calculations much easier. The old coins ceased to be accepted as currency.

3 — LOSING VALUE

After World War I (1914-18), the German government printed large amounts of notes to try to pump money back into the country. People felt richer, so they bought more goods. But the increased demand meant prices rose dramatically – by more than 1,000,000,000,000,000%!

⬆ This German banknote was worth ten million marks.

Connect!

WHY DO WE ALL USE DIFFERENT CURRENCIES? SEE Q44.

39 Can banks collapse?

Very occasionally, a bank can run out of money and collapse. Investors may lose some, or all, of their savings.

☆ A LOSS OF CONFIDENCE

People give their money to banks to look after – they invest it. As long as they are confident that the bank will give the money back when they ask for it, they will leave the money there until they need it.

IN THE FILM *MARY POPPINS* (1964), A CHILD ASKED FOR HIS COIN BACK FROM THE BANK. THIS STARTED A 'RUN' ON THE BANK – EVERYONE ELSE WANTED THEIR MONEY BACK TOO, AS THEY FEARED THE BANK WOULD NOT HAVE THE FUNDS TO PAY THEM ALL.

☆ BAD BUSINESS

IN 1991, THE BANK OF COMMERCE AND CREDIT INTERNATIONAL (BCCI) COLLAPSED WITH DEBTS OF AROUND $20 BILLION. THE BANK'S 30,000 INVESTORS LOST MOST, OR ALL, OF THEIR MONEY.

IN 1995, BRITAIN'S BARINGS BANK COLLAPSED WITH LOSSES OF OVER £800 MILLION. THE BANK WAS BROKEN BY ONE OF ITS OWN TRADERS, NICK LEESON, WHO HAD GAMBLED THE MONEY ON JAPANESE SHARES.

☆ LARGER BANKS MAY SUPPORT SMALLER ONES. IN 1985, THE CONTINENTAL BANK OF CANADA – THE SECOND LARGEST IN THE COUNTRY – WAS SAVED BY THE CENTRAL BANK PUMPING MONEY INTO IT.

Why are some countries rich and some poor?

The wealth of a country depends on how healthy, skilled and educated its people are, the resources it has and how the people use them. It also depends on the money that is available for building roads, factories and acquiring technology.

Trade

COUNTRIES NEED:
● GOOD TRANSPORT LINKS WITH THE REST OF THE WORLD.
● TO PRODUCE GOODS THAT ARE IN DEMAND.
● TO SELL GOODS AT A PRICE THAT IS COMPETITIVE.

IMPORTS = GOODS BOUGHT IN FROM OTHER COUNTRIES.

EXPORTS = GOODS SOLD TO OTHER COUNTRIES.

☆ WHO EXPORTS WHAT?

BOTSWANA = DIAMONDS
BRAZIL = COFFEE
BRUNEI = CRUDE OIL
CANADA = MINERALS
CHINA = RICE
CUBA = SUGAR
GHANA = COCOA BEANS
ISRAEL = CITRUS FRUIT
NEW ZEALAND = WOOL
NORWAY = TIMBER
JAPAN = CARS
PAKISTAN = COTTON
PORTUGAL = TEXTILES
RUSSIAN FEDERATION = COAL
USA = MACHINERY

☆ HOW RICH? HOW POOR?

A good way of examining the wealth of a country is to look at the number of luxury goods owned by its people. This chart shows how many people per 1,000 own a TV, car and telephone in three different countries.

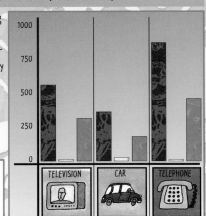

KEY
DENMARK
BURUNDI
BARBADOS

TELEVISION CAR TELEPHONE

Connect! COUNTRIES WITH FINANCIAL PROBLEMS MAY BORROW FROM MORE WEALTHY NATIONS. THIS CAN CREATE EVEN GREATER PROBLEMS. SEE Q41.

What do rich countries do to help poor ones?

Developing countries can borrow money from the developed world. Various kinds of aid are also given, such as food, medical supplies and new technology.

It is important to break the poverty cycle in some developing countries.

ADULT - - - - - → **0–6 MONTHS** - - - -
LITTLE MONEY, POOR DIET, BABY BORN UNDERWEIGHT
BABY WEAK AS MOTHER UNDERNOURISHED

6 MONTHS–5 YEARS
LACK OF SOLID FOOD, UNHYGIENIC LIVING QUARTERS

12–ADULT
POOR EDUCATION, LOW-PAID WORK

5–12 YEARS
LACK OF ENERGY, BAD PERFORMANCE AT SCHOOL

☆ NEW HOPE

Banks and governments in Western nations give loans to developing countries to help them set up new industries and improve existing ones.

BILATERAL AID = MONEY GIVEN BY ONE COUNTRY TO ANOTHER COUNTRY.

MULTILATERAL AID = MONEY GIVEN BY A GROUP OF COUNTRIES TO ANOTHER COUNTRY.

WORLD BANK = FOUNDED IN 1944 TO PROVIDE LOANS TO POORER NATIONS.

☆ THE PROBLEMS

● Many developing countries can not pay back the interest on the loan, let alone the original amount. The banks that lent them the money need to decide how to act.
● Aid may not reach the people in need. Many developing countries spend a great deal of money on defence, rather than reducing the poverty of their people.

☆ THE SOLUTIONS

● Western banks charging a lower rate of interest on loans, and reducing, or even cancelling, the debts owed by developing countries.
● Making it easier and more profitable for developing countries to sell their goods to the West.
● Developing countries should explore new industries and not rely on just one main export.

QUESTION

42 Can power create wealth?

Yes. For example in war, powerful, conquering nations have demanded heavy taxes from the people they have defeated. Sometimes they have imposed their own monetary systems. Rich nations may use their wealth to increase their power by paying for bigger armies and more advanced weapons.

☆ **PROVE IT!** ANSWERS: 20p; £4; £10; £20; £800,000.

1 Collecting taxes

☆ WHAT IS TAX?

Tax is an amount of money raised from individuals and organisations by a government, in order to pay for the services that it provides for the people. These services include street lighting, road maintenance and welfare benefits. Tax is usually charged on a person's income, property and goods bought. Some countries impose inheritance tax on money that is left to a person in a will.

Most people feel the tax they pay is too great, but there is usually little they can do to lower it. During the 11th century, Lady Godiva, from Coventry, England, asked her husband to reduce the city's heavy taxes. He agreed to do so – but only if she rode naked through the streets at noon! Lady Godiva bravely accepted the challenge, and the taxes fell.

Prove It!

Suppose there is a tax rate of 20%. How much tax would you have to pay on £1, £20, £50, £100, £4,000,000? To work it out, multiply each amount by 20 and divide by 100.
THE ANSWERS ARE HIDDEN ON THIS PAGE.

2 Imposing money systems

☆ THE FIRST NATIONAL COIN OF CHINA

In 221 BC, the state of Qin defeated the other six Chinese states of Chu, Zhno, Wei, Han, Yan and Qi. The victorious emperor, Shi Huangdi, replaced the many shapes of the existing Chinese coins with one shape: round, with a square hole in the middle.

THIS WAS A SYMBOLIC COIN. THE SQUARE HOLE REPRESENTED THE EARTH, WHILE THE ROUND COIN WAS THE HEAVENS. BY IMPOSING THIS COIN, THE EMPEROR BELIEVED HE WAS COMPLETING THE LINK BETWEEN HEAVEN AND EARTH. IN THIS WAY HE SHOWED HIS POWER.

☆ THE SIGN OF THE RULER

At the beginning of the 19th century, Napoleon Bonaparte (right) and his forces took control of Belgium and the Netherlands. The coins issued at this time were stamped with a letter N. This was a way of showing French authority.

☆ POWER OVER PEOPLE

IN 100 BC, THE CHINESE EMPEROR WU TI NEEDED MONEY. SO HE PUT ALL THE WHITE DEER IN THE AREA INTO THE ROYAL PARK, AND THEN DECLARED THAT ONLY PEOPLE WEARING WHITE DEERSKIN MASKS COULD ENTER THE PALACE. THE PEOPLE WERE FORCED TO BUY THE SKINS FROM THE EMPEROR, WHO CHARGED HUGE PRICES FOR THEM!

3 Money buys more power

☆ MONEY AND WAR

● Money buys weapons and pays for armies. Soldiers who fight for a foreign country are often paid large sums of money. They are called mercenaries.
● In the past, soldiers were recruited by being promised a share of the treasure, or booty, captured from the enemy.

⬆ European mercenaries fighting in Africa in 1961.

43

Can we tell how people lived by looking at their money?

Yes. The pictures and inscriptions on coins can tell us many things about a country: its history, its geography, its past and present rulers, its famous citizens and its achievements. The way money was used also tells us about how people lived.

Style and design

☆ PICTURING THE WORLD

Ancient Greek and Roman coins provide information about many aspects of their lives. Designs include animals, fish, trees, gladiator fights, soldiers, weapons, temples and gods.

COINS ARE ONE OF OUR BEST SOURCES OF INFORMATION ON WHAT ANCIENT CITIES LOOKED LIKE. WHILE THE BUILDINGS THEMSELVES MAY NOT HAVE SURVIVED, MANY COINS FEATURING THEM HAVE. ROMAN COINS SHOW ALMOST A THOUSAND DIFFERENT EXAMPLES OF ARCHITECTURE, FROM TEMPLES, LIGHTHOUSES AND FOUNTAINS TO BRIDGES, AQUEDUCTS AND CITY WALLS.

☆ PICTURING THE RULER

The Greeks did not believe in glorifying the individual. Their coins featured general images of royalty rather than portraits. Alexander the Great (356–323 BC) changed all that when he conquered Greece in 336 BC. He decided that it was appropriate to show rulers on coins and had coins minted showing his own face.

Inscriptions

☆ RULERS AND SLOGANS

The words stamped on ancient coins often include the names and titles of emperors, kings, queens and other heads of state. These inscriptions may include a slogan that gives us an insight into a country's history.

IN 1969, THE ZAMBIAN GOVERNMENT MINTED A 50-NGWEE COIN SHOWING A PICTURE OF AN EAR OF MAIZE AND THE SLOGAN 'GROW MORE FOOD FOR MANKIND'. IT WAS ENCOURAGING FARMERS TO INCREASE THEIR OUTPUT, BOTH FOR THE COUNTRY'S OWN USE AND FOR EXPORT PURPOSES.

THIS AMERICAN $1 COIN, FROM 1879, FEATURES 13 STARS AND THE LATIN INSCRIPTION 'E PLURIBUS UNUM'. THIS MEANS 'FROM MANY, ONE'. IT REFERS TO THE JOINING TOGETHER, IN 1787, OF THE ORIGINAL 13 COLONIES ON THE EAST COAST OF NORTH AMERICA TO FORM THE USA. THE ONE DOLLAR COIN CARRIES THE SAME DESCRIPTION TODAY.

How is the money spent?

☆ DENOMINATIONS

Sometimes, the only coins that are discovered for a particular ancient civilisation are those of a high value. This suggests that everyday buying and selling of low-priced goods was carried out using some form of barter.

☆ MAKING MONEY AND SPENDING IT

How people earn money and then spend it varies throughout the world.

CAPITALISM
THIS SYSTEM IS BASED ON INDIVIDUALS BEING FREE TO MAKE THEIR OWN CHOICES ON HOW THEY WILL EARN AND SPEND THEIR MONEY. PEOPLE ARE ENCOURAGED TO ACQUIRE WEALTH, POSSESSIONS AND PROPERTY, TO WORK FOR THEMSELVES AND TO RELY ON THE STATE AS LITTLE AS POSSIBLE.

COMMUNISM
IN THIS SYSTEM, THE STATE OWNS AND CONTROLS THE PRODUCTION OF ALL FOOD AND GOODS. TODAY, THE COMMUNIST SYSTEM EXISTS IN JUST A FEW COUNTRIES, INCLUDING CUBA AND NORTH KOREA. DECISIONS ARE TAKEN BY THE GOVERNMENT, RATHER THAN THE INDIVIDUAL.

Connect!

HOW DO PEOPLE USE MONEY TO SHOW WEALTH AND STATUS? SEE Q50.

Connect!

WHEN WE ARE ABROAD, HOW DO WE EXCHANGE OUR OWN MONEY WITH THAT OF ANOTHER COUNTRY? SEE Q45.

QUESTION

44

Why don't we all use the same currency?

The currency – banknotes and coins – that a country uses depends on many things: the materials available, the minting and printing techniques, and the history of that nation. Who ruled it? Did they impose their own currency? Have the present rulers changed the currency in any way?

1 CURRENCY DEVELOPS THROUGH TIME

● When buying and selling, people have to exchange something that they all agree is valuable. In Thailand, various parts of the tiger – such as claws, tail, teeth and tongue – were rare and treasured enough to be acceptable as money.

● In time, replicas of the tiger parts that were being exchanged were made and used instead.

● As trade grew beyond local transactions, the Thai people had to find a way of making their currency more hard-wearing and portable. They began to make durable coins made out of metal. Silver coins in the shape of a tiger's tongue were still being used as money until very recently.

2 CURRENCY IS AFFECTED BY WARS

Between the 15th and the early 20th centuries, European nations took power of many countries around the world. The rulers of these colonies often issued a new form of money. They based it on the existing currency, as they reasoned that people would not value what they did not recognise.

THE FRENCH ISSUED THEIR OWN SILVER COINS IN MADAGASCAR IN THE 19TH CENTURY. THE COINS WERE CUT UP BY THE LOCAL PEOPLE, WHO VALUED THE WEIGHT OF THE METAL MORE THAN THE COINS THEMSELVES!

3 GOVERNMENTS CONTROL CURRENCY

Governments prefer to keep control of the money circulating in their country themselves. They can do this more easily by having their own currency.

Worldwide currencies

☆ NORTH AMERICA

CANADA = DOLLAR
COSTA RICA = COLON
HAITI = GOURDE
MEXICO = PESO
USA = DOLLAR

☆ SOUTH AMERICA

ARGENTINA = PESO
CHILE = PESO
PARAGUAY = GUARANI
PERU = INTI
VENEZUELA = BOLIVAR

☆ AFRICA

ANGOLA = KWANZA
ETHIOPIA = BIRR
LIBYA = DINAR
MADAGASCAR = ARIARY
NIGERIA = NAIRA
SIERRA LEONE = LEONE
SOUTH AFRICA = RAND
TANZANIA = SHILINGI
ZAIRE = ZAIRE
ZAMBIA = KWACHA

☆ EUROPE

FRANCE = FRANC
FINLAND = MARKKA
GERMANY = MARK
GREECE = DRACHMA
IRELAND = PUNT
ITALY = LIRA
SWEDEN = KRONA
NORWAY = KRONA
POLAND = ZLOTY
PORTUGAL = ESCUDO
RUSSIA = RUBLE
SPAIN = PESETA
UK = POUND

☆ AUSTRALASIA

AUSTRALIA = DOLLAR
NEW ZEALAND = DOLLAR

☆ ASIA

AFGHANISTAN = AFGHANI
CHINA = YUAN
INDIA = RUPEE
JAPAN = YEN
KUWAIT = DINAR
MALAYSIA = RINGGIT
MONGOLIA = TUKHRIK
PHILIPPINES = PESO
SAUDI ARABIA = RIAL
SINGAPORE = DOLLAR
VIETNAM = DONG

Sharing a currency

After signing the Maastricht Treaty in 1991, the governments in the European Union (EU) used a common currency, ECU (right), to calculate their finances. Many European countries have now agreed to use a shared currency called the euro.

45 What is the exchange rate?

Visitors to another country usually need to exchange their money for the local currency. The amount of money they will receive will depend on the exchange rate. The exchange rate of one currency is a measure of the value of that currency against another one.

☆ SETTING A RATE

Exchange rates vary from day to day. They depend on how valuable each currency is, how it compares with other currencies and how much in demand the currency is internationally.

EVERY DAY, AROUND $1,000 BILLION-WORTH OF FOREIGN EXCHANGE TRANSACTIONS TAKE PLACE AROUND THE WORLD.

⬆ Different currencies are bought and sold on what is called the foreign exchange market.

☆ CUSTOMERS

● Large, powerful companies called multinationals need foreign currencies to trade with foreign countries. Most imported goods need to be paid for in the currency of the country of their origin.

● Banks buy and sell currencies. They talk about the exchange rate as being 'the number of dollars to the pound', 'the number of krona to the zloty', and so on.

● Brokers are people, or companies, who trade currencies on behalf of someone else. They make sure that they know which bank will buy a currency for the most money and sell it for the least.

THE MONEY IN YOUR POCKET
THIS TABLE SHOWS HOW MANY DOLLARS, MARKS AND YEN YOU WOULD GET FOR **ONE BRITISH POUND** DURING VARIOUS YEARS.

YEAR	US DOLLAR	GERMAN MARK	JAPANESE YEN
1920	3.66	404.59	7.6
1930	4.86	20.38	9.9
1940	4.03	11.98	16.8
1960	2.81	11.71	1,008.2
1980	2.33	4.23	525.6
1990	1.79	2.88	258.4
1997	1.66	2.65	196.29

Prove It!

Using the exchange rates shown in the table above, work out when would have been the best time to exchange pounds for yen. THE ANSWER IS HIDDEN ON THIS PAGE.

Connect!

WHAT WAS BLACK MONDAY? FIND OUT IN Q48.

46 How much money can you take in and out of a country?

A government controls the amount of money entering and leaving the country, because it needs to know how much money exists in the country at any one time.

☆ LOOKING AT THE LIMITS

COUNTRY	CURRENCY	MAXIMUM AMOUNT OF MONEY IN/OUT
BANGLADESH	TAKA	500
EL SALVADOR	COLON	200
ETHIOPIA	BIRR	10
ITALY	LIRA	20,000,000
BRAZIL	REAL	NO LIMITS

DO PEOPLE SMUGGLE MONEY? YES! IN THE USA, THE FEDERAL RESERVE SYSTEM (FRS) CONTROLS THE AMOUNT OF MONEY IN CIRCULATION AND THE AMOUNT BEING BORROWED. FRS OFFICIALS CANNOT TRACK DOWN ALL THE MONEY THAT HAS BEEN ISSUED. THEY FEAR THAT MORE THAN ONE-THIRD OF THE MISSING MONEY HAS BEEN SMUGGLED ABROAD.

QUESTION

47

Do we know how much money exists in the world?

No. The money supply is the total amount of money in circulation in a country at any time. It can be the cash in your pocket or the money deposited in banks and building societies. But, it is impossible to put a figure on how much actual money there is in the world.

☆ WHY DON'T WE KNOW?

● Not every country is able to maintain an accurate record of its money supply.
● People are not always honest about admitting how much money they have.
● People invest money in valuable goods, such as paintings and property. The values of such investments change constantly.
● Criminals forge and smuggle vast amounts of money around the world.

QUESTION

48

What is the stock exchange?

A stock exchange – also known as a stock market – is a place where goods in the form of stocks and shares are bought and sold.

QUESTION

49

Who decides how much money things are worth?

The value of anything is determined by the price someone will pay for it.

1

SHARES (OR EQUITIES)

Shares are bought by people who want to invest in a company. By owning shares, they own a part of the company. The value of the shares will depend on how well, or badly, the business performs. If it does well, the share price increases.

2

STOCKS (OR BONDS)

Stocks are sums of money lent to a government or large company. The money is paid back at some point in the future, with interest. Unlike shares, stocks do not give the person lending the money any ownership of the company.

⬆ In a stock exchange, the people who buy and sell stocks and shares on behalf of individuals or organisations are known by various names, including brokers, agents and marketmakers.

☆ WHAT WAS BLACK MONDAY?

On Monday 19 October 1987, share prices on the world's stock exchanges fell dramatically. The crash was caused by a sudden lack of confidence by investors in the economy. American markets lost $1,000 billion, while the London Stock Exchange lost £94 billion.

THE LARGEST STOCK EXCHANGES ARE IN NEW YORK, TOKYO AND LONDON.

☆ SETTING THE PRICE

Prices may be set by the owner, the manufacturer or by bidders at an auction house. The person who needs or wants the item must decide if they can afford it.

☆ THE MOST VALUABLE...

VIOLIN	A Stradivarius violin was auctioned at Christie's, London, England, in 1990. It fetched £902,000 ($1.5 million).
DIAMOND	In 1995, a 100-carat pear-shaped diamond was sold at Sotheby's, Geneva, Switzerland, for $16.5 million (£10.5 million).
PAINTING	Vincent van Gogh's *Portrait of Dr Gachet* (1890) was sold at Christie's, New York, USA, in 1991 for $82.5 million (£49.1 million).

Connect!

ARE THERE SAFER WAYS OF STORING WEALTH? SEE Q50.

50 How do people use money to show their wealth?

Each country has its own traditional symbols of wealth. Some people spend their money on clothes, food, cars and holidays. Others invest in items that they believe will become more valuable in the future, such as gold, jewellery, antiques and paintings.

COLLECTING THE RARE

STAMPS COLLECTING STAMPS CAN BE EXPENSIVE. A PENNY 1856 BRITISH GUIANA STAMP RECENTLY SOLD FOR $935,000.

FINE WINE SOME WINES CAN COST THOUSANDS OF POUNDS. IN 1985, A RECORD £105,000 WAS PAID AT AUCTION FOR A BOTTLE OF 1787 CLARET.

FURNITURE ANTIQUE FURNITURE IS SOUGHT AFTER FOR ITS WORKMANSHIP. RARE PIECES MAY COST THOUSANDS, EVEN MILLIONS, OF POUNDS.

SPENDING THE MOST

Hassanal Bolkiah Muizzaddin Waddaulah (the Sultan of Brunei) is one of the world's richest people. His 50th birthday party was held over three days in July 1996. It cost around **£17 million.**

POP STAR MICHAEL JACKSON WAS FLOWN IN AT A COST OF £10 MILLION TO GIVE THREE CONCERTS.

GUESTS FEASTED ON £6.5 MILLION OF FOOD AND NON-ALCHOLIC DRINK.

£500,000 WAS SPENT ON DECORATIONS AND FLORAL ARRANGEMENTS.

52 What will money be like in the future?

The future of money will depend on how we live and what people find valuable.

ELECTRONIC CASH (E-CASH)
SMART CARDS ARE ALREADY WIDELY USED IN BRITAIN, FRANCE AND OTHER COUNTRIES. THEY HAVE A TINY BUILT-IN COMPUTER CHIP THAT DEPLETES THE VALUE OF THE CARD EACH TIME IT IS USED. THE CHIP ALSO ALLOWS MORE CASH TO BE LOADED ONTO THE CARD WHEN IT IS INSERTED INTO A SLOT AT SPECIAL CREDIT POINTS.

BACK TO BARTER
SOME PEOPLE BELIEVE THAT WE ARE SLAVES TO MONEY: WE EARN, WE SPEND, WE BORROW, WE OWE. OTHERS THINK THAT IT IS TIME TO GO BACK TO A SYSTEM WHERE WE ARE NOT DEFINED BY HOW MUCH MONEY WE HAVE, BUT BY WHO WE ARE AND HOW WE SPEND OUR TIME. THEY BELIEVE WE SHOULD GO BACK TO BARTERING – EXCHANGING WHAT WE HAVE FOR WHAT WE NEED.

51 Has the world become obsessed by money?

Some people, particularly those in the Western world, have become preoccupied with making money and spending it. We even make films about money!

GOLDFINGER (1964), THE THIRD OF THE JAMES BOND FILMS, FEATURES THE VILLAINOUS GOLDFINGER. HE PLANS TO PLANT A BOMB IN FORT KNOX TO TRY TO CONTAMINATE THE USA'S HOARD OF GOLD! IF HE SUCCEEDS, IT WOULD INCREASE THE VALUE OF HIS OWN GOLD, WHICH HE AMASSED BY SMUGGLING.

☆ "I DON'T GET OUT OF BED FOR LESS THAN $10,000 A DAY" (LINDA EVANGELISTA, CANADIAN MODEL).

Connections!

⬤ Money, cash, currency – it really is just a medium of exchange, and yet it has the power to make people steal, lie and even murder. Could the world exist without money? Not until we find a way of making and distributing all the things we need to survive, without asking people to exchange money for them.

Connections!
MONEY
Index

☆ SYMBOLS USED IN THIS BOOK (UNLESS OTHERWISE STATED): $=US DOLLARS; £=UK POUNDS.